To Joelle, With Love

Letters to My Daughter

Kia Clark

ISBN 978-93-5667-571-1
© Kia Clark 2023

Published in India 2023 by Pencil

A brand of

One Point Six Technologies Pvt. Ltd.
Unit no. 26, Ground Floor, Building A1,
Wadala Truck Terminal Road,
Near Post Office, Antop Hill, Mumbai - 400037
E connect@thepencilapp.com
W www.thepencilapp.com

DISCLAIMER: *The opinions expressed in this book are those of the authors and do not purport to reflect the views of the Publisher.*

Author biography

I am Kia Clark, a passionate writer, interior decorator, and home cook, among other things. My primary role in life is that of a wife and mother, and my family keeps me busy, even as my children have grown older and less dependent.

As a creative person, I always find ways to express myself. Writing has been a form of therapy for me, and it is something I enjoy doing whenever I have some free time. I have never had formal training as a writer, but it is a love of mine that has allowed me to communicate my thoughts and feelings in a safe space.

My quiet personality has always made it difficult for me to express myself verbally, so I have taken to writing as a means of self-expression. I have always found writing to be a powerful tool for exploring my emotions and the world around me.

To Joelle, With Love: Letters to My Daughter is my first book, and it's a compilation of my written words. It is a passion project that I have been working on for some time now. I am excited to share my work with others and hope that it will inspire and touch their lives in some way.

CONTENTS

My Prayer For You 9

Your Birth Day 11

Memories Of My Mother 14

Who Is Joelle 16

What It Means To Be Thirteen 17

Young Love 19

Memories Are Forever 22

I Am More Than Your Mom 25

Dear J O E L L E 28

Birthdays Are Best Celebrated 30

2023 Playlist 32

We Are Your Village 34

Should You Ever Wonder... 36

You Are Officially A Teenger 38

P.S. I Love You 41

Generations of Great Women Surround You 43

Lessons I Have Learned 46

Your Feelings Matter 49

La La's Lessons 52

God Bless You 55

Your Dad Adores You 57

The World Needs You..59

10 Things You Need To Keep Doing..............................60

Brothers Are Not So Bad 63

Love Your Body...64

Be Encouraged 66

The Value of Friends..68

My Friend, Your Angel 70

Thirteen (BIG) Little Things...73

Always Remember... 76

Facts About My Favorite Daughter 77

Enjoy Each Day Of Every Year.....................................79

It Is True, It Is So 80

To The Future (23) You 81

List of Contributors...83

Acknowledgements

Happy 13th Joelle!!! This book is dedicated to you, my precious Baby Girl, and I hope it brings you as much joy and wisdom as it did for me writing it. I love you more than words could ever express!

To Alita, Nikki, and Toni - I cannot thank you enough for being my unwavering support system, pushing me to keep writing and not let my fear hold me back from putting myself out there. You truly understood the assignment of being a supportive circle, and for that, I am forever grateful.

To every amazing lady who contributed to this book by taking the time to write to Joelle, I cannot express my gratitude enough - THANK YOU!!! Your willingness to share your experiences and insights without hesitation is a testament to the incredible bond we share as a tribe, and I feel blessed beyond measure to have you all in my life.

Introduction

In 2020, the world came to a standstill due to the COVID-19 pandemic. For many of us, this unexpected downtime gave us the chance to reflect on our lives and spend time with loved ones. As for me, I found myself journaling more than ever before. With my kids' constant activity, life before the pandemic was always on the go, leaving me little time for introspection. However, as the world slowed down, I had the chance to take in my 13-year-old daughter in a new way.

What I discovered surprised me - she was me. It was like looking in a mirror, and it got me thinking about what I needed to hear and know when I was her age. The truth is, at her age, I felt alone in my pubescent and teenage experiences, and I know now that I was not alone. So, I began to journal memories and life lessons that I felt would be useful for my daughter, writing to her was easy because the young girl still resided inside of me.

Eventually, what started as a personal journal transformed into a book that I believe will make a great keepsake. This book highlights my daughter's 13th year, but the life lessons and stories shared are relevant and can be referenced at any age. To make this book even more meaningful, I asked other women in my daughter's life to write to her as well. Their contributions elevated this book beyond what I ever imagined. My hope is that this book serves as a source of encouragement and upliftment for not just my daughter but for other women who read it as well.

However, I want to make it clear that I am not an expert. I am just a mom who has experienced life, and the advice, thoughts, beliefs, and opinions that I share in this book come from my personal experiences. Each contributor to this book should be extended the same disclaimer, and I urge readers to seek professional advice for emotional issues and well-being.

So, to my daughter and to every woman who reads this book, I say, "Read up, buttercup!" and may the stories and lessons shared inspire you to embrace life and all its challenges.

XOXO,
Mom

My Prayer For You

I claim victory over your life, knowing that you are more than a conqueror through Christ who strengthens you. May you always remember that no weapon formed against you shall prosper and that you are protected from all hurt, harm, and danger.

May you experience the fullness of health and wholeness in every area of your life. Physically, mentally, emotionally, and financially, I pray that you thrive and live life abundantly.

May your circle be filled with people who love you with the unconditional love described in 1 Corinthians 13. May they support and encourage you in all your endeavors, and may you be a source of love and encouragement for them as well.

May your heart always be humble and may you give God the glory in all things. I pray that your every need is supplied so that you can accomplish your aspirations and goals. May your purpose and calling be revealed to you, and may you walk confidently in it.

May you see yourself the way that God sees you. One of a kind. Beautifully and wonderfully made. Worthy and deserving of his goodness. May you live by the Golden Rule and treat others the way you want to be treated. Share kindness. Show love.

May you take notice of the wonder in the little things, and may you always control your temper and not give full vent to people and situations that negatively affect you.

May your faith be steadfast even in hard times. Because God will never fail you or give you more than you can bear. May you grant yourself the same grace, love, and forgiveness that God gifts you, and may you be bold and confident in who you are and whose you are.

I pray all of these things over your life, knowing that God's plans for you are good and that he will never leave you or forsake you. May you walk in victory and live a life that honors and glorifies him.

In Jesus' name, Amen.

Your Birth Day

Dear Joelle,

My beautiful, kind, gorgeous, loving, and athletic niece. You are so talented in so many aspects of your life, at 13 years old, and I am very proud of you. I feel so privileged your mom asked me to write in your 13-year-old coming-out book. You are indeed a deserving, loving spirit. You were my first live birth. I have three children but I was always on the other end. When your mom asked me if I would be in the delivery room with her it touched my heart, therefore, you will always touch my heart.

Let me tell you about your birth experience. Kia was in so much pain but they gave her the epidural and that seem to calm her down a lot. It was a happy and sad occasion because we were all missing Ma Ma. We knew you were a special gift from heaven. After a few hours of sitting around talking (me, Aunt Robin, Aunt Nikki, and Dr. Jen- the doctor), Aunt Robin had to make a call to her job. Then.........everything went into action. All of a sudden, I guess you started coming down the birth canal because nurses flew into the room, and lights dropped out of the ceiling. The nurses were prepping the birthing bed and the leg rest came out of the bottom of the bed. Everything was in Go Go Go mode. I was so in awe of everything around me. Then your little head with so much hair, that you have had from the moment you came into this world, popped out. You have always been absolutely beautiful. Well as a toddler, we could not even look at you without your bursting into tears. Then all of a sudden, you became Ms. Personality.

Jo Jo, I want you to remember that you are very special. Anything you want in life is yours, you just have to go after it. In life, you will get ups and downs but the downs are what teach you how to be stronger. I want you to journal every day and set goals every year. I wish someone would have told me, at the age of 13, not to take life too seriously. Everything will pass. Choose whatever career in life will make me happy and you will never feel like you are working. You will probably go through several careers until you find the right one. Always do your best and strive for excellence. When you purposely strive for excellence is when you will win, each and every time. I love you beyond measure.

I ask God right now to speak favor over your life. This is my prayer for you: Father in heaven, we praise your name, and we are thankful for all the blessings you have given us as a family. We thank you so much for allowing us to have Joelle in our lives. She is such a special, kind, beautiful spirit. Father in heaven, we ask that you watch over her every day of her life and guide her correctly. Allow her to always see that she is beyond extraordinary. Awesome. We ask that you allow your angels to surround her every day of her life and keep her from any harm, any obstacles that make a tear, or cause her to feel defeated. Father in heaven, we ask that you allow Joelle to always look in the mirror and see the beautiful, kind, loving person that is inside of her each and every day, each and every time, each and every way. Thank you for allowing Kia and Maceo to be excellent parents for Joelle. Father in heaven, we ask these things in Jesus Christ's name, Amen. Amen. Amen.

Also, your grandmother is in heaven, watching over you. She will never let you fail and always let you conquer. She was so excited that a little girl was going to be born so she could spoil her. But I believe she is spoiling you in heaven.

Love,
Auntie Lita

Memories Of My Mother

Early Life: My mother was named after her mother, Dorothy, and her paternal aunt, Lena. Her nickname was Sister, given to her by Aunt Viv who would introduce her as "my sister". She was born in May, one day before her mother's birthday (the 10th day of her birth month just like you), and was the second oldest of four children. She stood at an impressive 5'10", taller than the average woman. She had a gap between her front teeth for years an her hair color was either blonde, auburn, or brunette.

Memories: Growing up, I have vivid memories of my mother watching the student quiz show *It's Academic* on Saturday mornings. She owned four cars over her lifetime, including a yellow Mercury Cougar, a red Nissan Datsun, a blue Chevrolet Corsica, and a silver Toyota Camry that I inherited after her passing. One of the most hilarious things she did was pretending to sing opera. She allowed me to sleep in her bed until an age that I refuse to admit, and she always had her camera ready to take pictures.

Favorites: My mother had a few favorite movies, including *Imitation of Life*, *Mahogany*, and *Lady Sings the Blues*. She loved Diana Ross and Billy Dee Williams. Her favorite holiday was Christmas, and she decorated her home beautifully every year. Fried chicken was her favorite food, specifically chicken breast. One of her last requests was a piece of fried chicken. She loved baking, and her strawberry shortcakes, banana pudding, sweet potato pies, and brownies were the best. Her favorite color was red, and she adored babies.

Personality: My mother was a tough woman who never backed down from anyone, regardless of age or gender. The most gangster thing I ever witnessed was her standing in front of a car and daring the driver to hit her. She was also strong-willed and quit smoking cigarettes cold turkey. She was a great confidant, always giving the best advice. She never told you what you wanted to hear but what you needed to hear.

My mother was not just a parent but also a friend. Losing her was one of the hardest things I have ever experienced. She left me with a void that seems impossible to fill. I wish I could bring my mother back to life so that you could experience her. Although I know that is impossible, I hope sharing these facts about her helped you feel closer to her.

XOXO,
Mom

Who Is Joelle

Who is Joelle?

*She is precious as a jewel.

*She is Kind, Beautiful, and Brilliant with unmatched self-confidence.

*She is her Mom's "Mini-me"

*She is her Dad's Princess, holding the strings to his heart.

*She is her Brothers "Favorite" Sister.

*She is Loved & Adored by her FAMILY.

SHE IS A TREASURE BEYOND COMPARE!

We Love You, Joelle,
Aunt Gail & Aunt Courtney

What It Means To Be Thirteen

Thirteen. That is a big year because you get to make some big discoveries about yourself and who you want to be. Your entire future is right there- so close! You can start to grab pieces of it every day. So many exciting things will happen over the next few years and you will want to rush to get to each of them.

If I can go back and talk to myself when I was thirteen- I would tell myself two things. First, do not rush! Everything will happen in good time and there is no reason to look towards the future when the present is so exciting. I would tell myself that 13 brings new experiences, new friends, and new emotions. Trying to rush into 14, 15, and 16 means that I missed so many of the wonderful parts of being 13. Boys can still be gross (that will stay the truth well into adulthood) and sleepovers can still involve cartoons and scary stories. Spend all the time you can with your mom because she is so cool and you will learn so much from her. Do not rush to the next step, because when you get there- you will miss what you left.

Second, and MOST IMPORTANT, Ask. For. Help. So much heartache could have been avoided if I just asked for help. Thirteen is hard because so much is new and maybe people changed when you have not yet. Your mom, dad, older siblings, aunts, uncles- they all went through this. If I just could have reached out for help when I was struggling, I could have learned that what I was feeling was normal and common. I thought I was the only one who struggled with confidence, and everyone else felt "cool" and "pretty". But that is not true at all. No one can survive alone forever. I was blessed with an amazing, supportive family- JUST LIKE YOU. I did not rely on them, because I was independent and stubborn. But boy do I rely on them now. So when you struggle, do not think about it. Ask. For. Help.

And maybe the last piece of advice I would give you, and it is not really advice so I am not going to number it, is to take your crown off and put it on the shelf for safekeeping. Joelle- you are a QUEEN. But that crown is heavy and it will weigh you down. So take it off and keep it safe, so you can run through life without worrying about it. The time to wear it will come. But as you know, you do not need to wear that crown to be the queen that you are. Everyone knows from your beauty that shines from the inside out.

Love you, Joelle! Every single time I have seen you, from when you were a preschooler to a middle schooler- you always greeted me with a smile and a big hug. I told your parents many times that you are my favorite Clark and that is not a lie. You are pure joy, pure love. Continue to boss your dad and brothers around and know every day that your mother's heart became full from your brothers but grew the day that you were born.

Mrs. Linda

Young Love

It is perfectly normal to be curious about love and relationships, even if you are not yet allowed to date. These experiences are an important part of growing up and maturing, and it is natural for them to be on your mind. Despite my seeming ancient to you (eye roll), I remember my middle and high school days. Crushes and "love" interests were just as common a topic as our coursework. I recall feeling so unsure of myself, wondering if the person I was crushing on even noticed me or would like me back, whether I would be able to keep up a conversation with them, or if I would be too shy to even say a word. Believe me, when I tell you, I know all too well the feeling of uncertainty and confusion that comes with having a crush. It is easy to feel like you are the only one who does not know what to say or how to act around your crush. But the truth is, many of your peers are likely experiencing similar doubts and anxieties. So if you are feeling lost or unsure, please know that you are not alone, and it is perfectly okay to take your time and figure things out at your own pace.

Here is what I want you to always remember WHEN you start dating:

It is important to meet people and learn what you like and dislike. Take the time to flirt, converse, and go out to do fun activities without rushing into exclusivity. Remember to hold on to your virginity, as it is precious and can never be regained once lost. You have your entire life to explore sexual experiences, so there is no need to rush into anything.

Remember that you are the guardian of your body, and you have the final say in what happens to it. Do not feel pressured or bullied into doing anything that makes you uncomfortable. Always trust your intuition-if it feels wrong, then it is. Be cautious when sharing intimate details (written words, photos, videos) with someone. Ensure that the person is trustworthy and has integrity. Do not compromise your values or boundaries for the sake of a relationship. You are worthy of love and respect, and the right person will recognize and appreciate that.

Dating at any age can be both heartwarming and hard, full of ups and downs. Disagreements and mistakes will happen and are okay. However, every mishap should not be treated as an accident, as some mess-ups are intentional acts of deceit and disloyalty that can lead to heartbreak. Heartbreak is inevitable, but it is something that you can learn from and eventually heal from.

In the event that a relationship ends, it is essential to move on and not allow someone to play with your feelings. Although it can be challenging, walking away will save you from more significant pain later on. Additionally, authenticity is critical in any relationship. Always be yourself, and do not pretend to be someone you are not. Not everyone will like you, and that is perfectly fine. The right person will come along who will appreciate you for who you are.

Finally, always know that you can talk to me about anything. Even if you do not think I can relate or feel comfortable discussing a particular topic with me, I am here for you. I would rather us talk about it than not talk about it at all. Remember that I love you and want the best for you.

XOXO,
Mom

Memories Are Forever

Dear Sweet Joelle,

When the announcement was made that your mom was having a baby girl, excitement filled the air. Everyone started suggesting names. My favorite was Popscicle (Jace's suggestion). Did you know I was your very first babysitter? And when you started calling me Grandma Ada my heart could have burst with joy!

My memories from babysitting you are:

1. "Break Every Chain" by Tasha Cobbs Leonard playing on the car radio and you broke out singing every word in such a sweet voice. A songstress was born that day. My other favorite songs that you sang were from the movie *Frozen* and "Roar" by Katy Perry.

2. We had a daily routine. After storytime came nap time, then watching a little television. But let's not forget going to the playground and having such a good time until, one day, that monkey (a pole) jumped in your way causing a knot on your head that scared me so bad.

3. Do you remember playing dress-up? You and Kobi would design, make, and model paper wedding gowns.

4. When playing school we would use La La's stuffed dolls and animals as students. Cayden would join us for school sessions. While La La would fall out laughing at our shenanigans.

5. I still remember looking around the house for tiny gloves to fit your little hands so you could collect leaves and start your first garden.

6. Short walks, treasure hunts, learning to ride your bike, board games, and snowball fights were always fun.

7. Let's not forget the food. It was shocking how you could devour Popeyes' chicken wings. Do you remember cracking eggs for baked goods and making breakfast to be served in our pretend restaurant? I sure do, I will never forget our famous tea parties and the mess that we made.

Your family lived in my home for a while. I loved it when you got bored with them and came to visit me. Oh, what happy times.

All these memories are my favorite things. I hope you have some favorite memories of us too. Most of all Joelle, I am grateful to God and your parents for sharing you with me. We had so much fun. And I thank you for the memories.

Trust God in all things and He will direct your path.

I love you,
Grandma Ada

Trust God in all things and He will direct your path.

I love you,
Grandma Ada

I Am More Than Your Mom

Have you ever felt like you knew someone your whole life, yet there was still so much you did not know about them? I want you to meet Kia, someone that you had known your entire life but is now being introduced to in a new way.

First and foremost, I am a child of God. My faith is the foundation of my life, and I am continually in awe of His unconditional love and favor for me. I am grateful for the gift and honor of being entrusted with my children, who are the best parts of me. They have been easy to raise and even easier to love, and I am beyond blessed to have them in my life.

Growing up in a home with both my mother and grandmother, taught me the importance of family and the value of strong relationships. Being born and bred in Baltimore gave me a distinct accent, I will not apologize for my dialect. I grew up on the Westside of Baltimore, where I spent most of my time -attending school, church, and social events. "Living in the hood," taught me tough lessons but never turned me into a fighter. I would much rather walk away from a physical altercation than throw hands. That being said, Mama Bear does not play about Papa Bear or her cubs.

I am a listener more than a talker, and I rarely ask for advice. Instead, I prefer to talk through my problems with the people I trust. Smiling comes naturally to me, and I have been asked countless times, "What are you smiling for?" or "Why are you always smiling?" Peopling can be draining for me, and I often prefer the solitude of home. Reading and decorating are two of my all-time favorite hobbies, and I also enjoy cooking. Interestingly enough, I did not learn to cook until well after I was married but I have since become quite good at it.

I am a crier, and simply watching a movie, reading a book, or hearing a touching story can cause me to shed a tear. When I moved out at 23, I cried for a month straight, even though I only moved 12 minutes away. I have never picked up cursing and opt not to drink as most alcohol tastes like cough syrup to me. I have never smoked cigarettes or done any type of drugs, and my interaction with the law does not extend beyond a traffic violation.

Sometimes, my emotions get the better of me, and I can be petty, hold a grudge, shut down, and detach. I am a Scorpio through and through. I embrace all aspects of my personality, both good and bad.

13 things that bring joy to my soul. These include hot food, string/fairy lights, summertime, R&B music, the smell of wet soil after it rains, pizza and french fries, the color blue, vacationing, cozy blankets, candles, reading, strawberry shortcake, and naps.

XOXO,
Mom

Dear J O E L L E

Dear Joelle,

As you move into your teenage years, I want you to celebrate and embrace the beautiful and unique individual that you are! As you journey from a teen to a young woman, remember to:

1. Always let your light shine and do not dim it for anyone (Matthew 5:16)

2. Make your plans but leave room for God to change them. (Proverbs 16:3)

3. Take one day at a time and enjoy every single day. (Matthew 6:11)

4. Take time for self-care even as you help others. (Mark 12:31)

5. Do your best always and God will do the rest. (Colossians 3:23)

Finally, as you celebrate your 13th birthday and beyond, remember to always remain J-O-E-L-L-E:

J: Joyful
O: Optimistic
E: Enthusiastic
L: Ladylike
L: Loving
E: Extraordinary

With Much Love,
Grandma Michelle

Birthdays Are Best Celebrated

Birthdays are special occasions that allow you to celebrate the gift of life, reflect on the past year's experiences, and look forward to the future with hope and optimism. No matter how big or small, every birthday celebration is an opportunity to create unforgettable memories that will last a lifetime. I want to share some of my most memorable birthday celebrations and why birthdays are worth celebrating.

Childhood Memories
As a child, I had the privilege of celebrating my birthdays with my family and closest friends. Some of my most vivid childhood memories include my McDonald's party, costume party, and sleepover. The McDonald's party was a classic 90s birthday celebration that involved eating hamburgers, playing on the playground, and meeting Ronald McDonald. The costume party was a Halloween-themed birthday celebration where my friends and I dressed up in our favorite costumes, had a costume contest, and played games. The sleepover was a cozy and fun-filled night where my friends and I watched movies, ate popcorn, and slept on the living room floor in our sleeping bags.

Adult Celebrations

As an adult, my most memorable birthday celebration was my 30th. My husband, family, and closest friends planned a surprise party at Angelina's, a popular restaurant and bar. It was a night of good food, drinks, music, and dancing. DJ Kaymoney kept the party going, and everyone had fun on the dance floor. I felt loved and appreciated, and the memories from that night will always hold a special place in my heart.

Why Birthdays are Worth Celebrating
Birthdays are worth celebrating for several reasons. First, your birthday is the date divinely chosen to present the gift of YOU to the world. It marks the beginning of your journey on earth and the many experiences that shape your life. Second, much was gained the day that you were born. Your birth brought joy, love, and happiness to your family and friends. Third, because there is and will only ever be one YOU. You are unique and special, and your birthday is a reminder of that. Fourth, your birthday is an extraordinary day. It is a day that is all about you, and it is a chance to indulge in the things that make you happy. Finally, birthdays are worth celebrating because they allow you to reflect on how far you have come and how much you have accomplished.

So on your next birthday, take the time to celebrate and make the most of the special day. Remember, you are cherished, loved, and appreciated, and your birthday is a reminder of that.

XOXO,
Mom

2023 Playlist

CUFF IT // Beyoncé
Flowers // Miley Cyrus
In Ha Mood // Ice Spice
Drake & 21 Savage // Rich Flex
Just Wanna Rock // Lil Uzi Vert
Snooze // SZA
I Hate You // SZA
Don't Play Wit It // Lola Brooke
Players // Coi Leray
Free Mind // Tems
ICU // Coco Jones
Bad Habit // Steve Lacy
F.N.F. // Glorilla

13 songs that will always remind you of your 13th year! Anytime you play any of these songs it will remind you of the fun things going on at this time, I am sure you know them all! I know you have heard older people saying "y'all don't know nothing bout this" when they hear music from their youth (rap, oldies, slow jams) LOL now you have your very own playlist of songs for when you get older.

Speaking of older… do not rush it! I remember when I was becoming a teenager I could not WAIT to be an adult. It just seemed more fun than having to go to school and do homework. I did not realize that everything is a process and that I will eventually get there with time. So instead, make sure you stay involved in school activities, make many memories with your friends-keep them around, dance, laugh, have fun, and just take it one year at a time. Do not compare yourself to anyone you are a star the way you are!

Taylor <3

We Are Your Village

Dearest Joelle,

I am so excited and honored to be able to share such an exciting time with you. When presented with the opportunity, I looked forward to it. It made me think back to when I met you. As I reflect on you back then, you were not just this cute energetic little girl in elementary school who would always be at her big brothers' soccer games, practices, and tournaments, you were this bright shining star!! Although you were small, you have always had this big personality. That is what stood out to me and seems to draw others to you. As you turn 13, I hope that you realize the impact that you have had and will continue to have on others. Effortlessly, people are drawn to your personality, your smile, your wit and all that is "Joelle." As you embark on these teenage years, know that it will be a time of laughter, excitement, and fun, as you get a little bit more freedom to express yourself and "do you." But, it will also be a time of learning, decisions, and transformation, as you come into your own and begin to balance more responsibility.

Always remember that you have a ton of people in your corner who are there to make sure that the best comes out of you. We are your village. People say that all of the time, right? It takes a village to raise a child. That does not mean that we scold you, when your parents are not near or that we have the authority to be your parent. It simply means that we are an extension of love, care, and concern. We want the best for you and will forever be there to cheer you on, hear you out, and support you.

Continue to be your best self!! I am proud to be in your village! Happy 13th Birthday!!

Ms. Terri

Should You Ever Wonder...

As you go through life, you may question your worth. You may feel like you fall short in certain areas, and that can lead to self-doubt and low self-esteem. But the truth is, you have unique qualities that make you special and valuable. It is important to recognize and celebrate those qualities in yourself.

First and foremost, you are loved. You may not always feel it or see it, but there are people in your life who care deeply for you. Whether it is family, friends, or even acquaintances, there are people who appreciate and admire you for who you are (read this book as proof). Take the time to reflect on those relationships and cherish the love that surrounds you.

Next, you are brave. Bravery does not mean you are never afraid or never face challenges. It means you have the courage to face your fears and overcome obstacles. You have shown bravery in many situations, whether it was getting stitches in your chin or completing your track heat after you fell. You have the strength and resilience to persevere through difficult times.

Creativity is a gift that allows you to express yourself in unique and meaningful ways. You have a talent for design, whether it is building houses in Bloxburg or creating trendy hairstyles. You have a unique eye and a creative spark that makes you stand out.

Talent is something that you often associate with natural abilities, but it is also something that can be developed through hard work and dedication. You have shown your talent in many areas, from setting personal records in track to teaching yourself how to do knotless braids. Your determination and effort have paid off, and you should be proud of your accomplishments.

Being capable means having the skills and resources to handle whatever comes your way. You have shown time and time again that you are capable of achieving great things. Whether it is excelling in school or taking on new challenges, you have the confidence and ability to succeed.

Finally, intelligence comes in many forms. You may not excel in every subject, but you have your own distinctive strengths and abilities. Your report cards reflect your hard work and dedication, and your willingness to improve shows your intelligence in its own right.

Should you ever wonder if you are enough, remember this: you are loved, brave, creative, talented, capable, intelligent, and much more. You are an extraordinary individual, and you should rejoice in the qualities that make you who you are. Embrace your strengths, work on your weaknesses, and know that you are loved and appreciated.

XOXO,
Mom

You Are Officially A Teenger

Dear Joelle,

CONGRATULATIONS!!! You are stepping into a new phase of life and of womanhood. You are 13!!! I remember turning 13 way back in the day (lol). It was a big deal. We were excited to be "off the clock". You know, that was back when we had to tell time on an actual round clock with hands and numbers...in the old days.

But you are "officially" a teenager now. No more kid or tween. And honestly, it is a big deal and a blessing. I struggled a bit when I was 13 and if I could tell my 13-year-old self a few things that I think would have been helpful in my maturation, here is what I would say:

1. Stand your ground - Peer pressure is a real thing and teenagers are relentless. Do not bend for anyone. Especially when you know that the end result will be hurtful to you or others.

2. Know who you are and allow yourself to grow and evolve. Evolution is inevitable and that is how God intends it for us.

3. Do not get stuck on any one thing to the point where it consumes you from sunup to sundown. It

is ok to like things and people and stuff but do not let it become an obsession. Do not lose yourself in it.

4. Be kind - Kindness never hurt anybody...period.

5. He is not the love of your life. LOL...I know you have found that boy that you think at this point could be the love of your life. You have scribbled his name on your papers with hearts and stars (at least that is what I did at your age lol). And that is ok. But do not plan that wedding yet.

6. Be a loyal but smart friend. You are a smart young lady so I am sure you will be able to see and feel when someone is trying to take advantage of you or your friendship. Trust your instincts.

7. Have Fun - You are young and free...enjoy your youth, teens, young adult years, and adult years. Live your life with no regrets.

8. Have a genuine and open relationship with God. Do not be intimidated by prayer. Talk to God like you talk to family or friends. He hears you and will talk back to you. As you mature you will recognize his voice and be able to clearly hear him.

9. Take pride in being a beautiful black girl. I cannot say it enough...you are BEAUTIFUL!!! Do not let anyone ever, EVER tell you differently. And if they try, send them to me!!!

10. Try new things, foods, experiences, etc. Do not always order chicken fingers and fries. You

cannot say you do not like something if you have never tried it.

11. Do everything in your power to achieve your goals. Nothing beats a failure but a try. Set those goals and do what you can do to make them your reality.

12. As you get older and make your own money, treat yourself. It does not have to be big purchases (although those are nice too). Order that extra dessert or get the appetizer AND the entree AND the dessert. Do not slight yourself.

13. And finally, and most important (in my opinion), love yourself. Society and social media will try to make you believe that you are not loved or you do not deserve love. But as long as you love yourself unconditionally, the world cannot tell you any different.

Joelle, you were born into families of strong, beautiful women who love hard and deep. God makes no mistakes and that is why you fit right in. Now it is time for you to take the world by storm. Show them who you are. And if they have any questions, tell them to talk to your Aunties...all of us. I love you to life and am super, super proud of who you are and who you will be. I cannot wait to see it.

Love Always and Forever,
Aunt Nikki

P.S. I Love You

My Ells,

I want to take a moment to tell you how much I love you. From the moment you entered this world, I knew that you were something special. You are everything that I never knew I needed, and you have brought so much joy and love into my life.

You were conceived during a time of mourning, and being pregnant with you helped me through a period of grief. Taking care of you once you were born allowed me to focus on something besides my loss. You were my comfort and my light during a difficult time, and you still are today.

We have always had a strong bond, from the first three years of your life when I stayed home to take care of you, to now. You have always been my sidekick (my literal day one), and I cannot imagine my life without you in it. Watching you grow up and experience new things has been a pleasure, and I am so proud of the person you have become.

I see so much of myself in you, from your creativity to how often there is a smile on your pretty face. You are not afraid to take risks and try new things, and I admire that about you. You have a tiger's heart (think Katy Perry's "Roar" lyrics), and I know that you will accomplish great things.

In the word of Burno Mars, "you're amazing just the way you are," (wink) and I love you more than words can express. Thank you for being a constant source of love, light, and joy in my life.

XOXO,
Mom

Generations of Great Women Surround You

Hey Joelle,

It is me, Aunt Robin! First, let me explain how I became Aunt Robin. I am not your mom's sister in the true sense of the word, but we grew up together and neither of us has a sister. Your mom is one of the very special people in my life who is as close as a sister could be. It was an honor for me when her kids came along and y'all graced me with the title Aunt Robin.

It has always been the most amazing thing how tight-knit our family is, and I want to share with you how much the women of our family have influenced my life. My memories all start with La La or Grandma Dot (that is what I called her). She was a God-fearing, strong, confident, loving, and supportive black woman. The family was always very, very important to her. She was the lady that whatever you needed if she could help you in any way you could consider it DONE!! I can remember, her opening her heart and home to my entire family. Even down to letting me, Uncle Nate, and Mya come to live with her. (I think that even played a part in us opening our home to others). She taught her kids to be the same way and we see this throughout our family. We all know how to show up and show out!!! From your Aunt Viv to Aunt Sister (your grandmother), to my mom (your Aunt Ada), and since I am talking about the women, even your Aunt Gail (who married your Uncle Brother, she came along and fit right in) they have always carried on the tradition of putting family first. It is their support and encouragement that always make me feel like I can accomplish anything. They have had my back and that is something you will be able to count on too! We will always be here for you!

Joelle, you have grown so much. Thinking of the PAST, you were a beautiful baby girl who stayed attached to your mom's hips, you were quiet and very observant, watching everything around you. Now as I look at you in the PRESENT, I see how you have blossomed into this, outgoing, always smiling (looking like your mom), smart, and talented young lady. It is amazing how you have come out of your shell. You are braiding your own hair, decorating your room, baking, running track, developing your own fashion sense, enjoying your TikTok dances, and drinking non-alcoholic Rose'. When I think of your FUTURE, I already know that you are gonna use that talent and intellect to do something GREAT!! I pray that you will go places and see things that you never even imagined. I pray that you will have a family of your own, a job that you love, and that you will be able to live comfortably. When you start to take steps towards that part of your life, just remember to put God first and your family second. Make sure to always love yourself. You can be or do ANYTHING and I can't wait to see what tomorrow will bring.

I Love You, Joelle!!!!!!
Aunt Robin

Lessons I Have Learned

Life lessons are the teachings that you get from the mistakes you make in life. Having lived a few decades, I have accumulated a good number of life lessons that I want to share with you. My goal is to help you avoid unnecessary struggles, anxieties, and stresses by learning from my experiences. If you choose to use my "life lessons," I will be more than happy to have passed the baton (you see what I did there lol) - but if you choose not to follow them (and make your own mistakes), just know I will still be here to support and guide you.

- The *Lord's Prayer* and the *Serenity Prayer* cover just about any situation or circumstance.

- It is your birthright to evolve and grow. You can and WILL outgrow people, places, and things.

- No. That is it, the complete sentence. No explanation, justification, or guilt is needed.

- By not making a decision, you have made a decision -so be sure to make your choice wisely.

- Failing does not make you a failure, it simply means you did not succeed at it THIS time.

- You can be your greatest ally or worst critic, be your own best friend.

- Your ex is your X for a reason, leave the past in the past.

- Love requires action. Pay more attention to deeds than words.

- Alone and loneliness are completely different. You can feel isolated in a crowded room and content in your own company.

- Gratitude never goes out of style, and it does not cost a thing. Be gracious.

- Invest in yourself -time, money, and energy. No one can advocate for you like you.

- Your body and business are personal, be selective about who you share them with.

- Non-negotiables are not to be negotiated, you compromise yourself and your integrity when doing so.

- Some people will not have the capacity to love you the way you need to be loved. It is not your fault or theirs, it just is.

- Take accountability for your wrongdoings, accidental or intentional. You have a better chance of being forgiven if you own up to your mistakes with sincerity.

- Trust your intuition, your gut feelings will not lead you wrong.

- Be optimistic, you will be happier and healthier.

- You are a whole and complete person with or without your mate. Love yourself most.

- Home is much more than physical space. If you keep your home close to your heart, you will always feel at home no matter where you are.

- A mother shares enough love to last beyond her lifetime so cherish every moment and absorb as much of it as you can.

XOXO,
Mom

Your Feelings Matter

Mental health is just as important as your medical health. When you are sick or injured, it is important to get the help that you need. Well, the same is true about mental health. What is mental health? It is part of your well-being that has to do with how you are feeling, thinking, coping, and adjusting to life changes.

How will you know if you are mentally healthy? Good mental health means that you are able to handle and navigate stress, pressure, change, disappointment, and other intense issues relatively well. Of course, you might cry, feel upset, get sad, or feel angry. This is normal! It's just your body's way of letting you know that something is wrong. But you're able to express your emotions, get support from family or friends, cope with it, and move on.

How do you know if your mental health is not in a good place? If you are struggling with mental health, you might feel constantly sad, worried, isolated, unmotivated, confused, struggling with low self-esteem, unable to focus, or not enjoying things you used to. You might be irritable, your grades might drop, and you might be feeling hopeless. We all have bad days, but if these feelings .last for more than a week or two, it is important to let your parents know that you are not feeling well. If you don't want to tell them what's wrong or you don't know or understand what's wrong, that's okay. They could schedule you to talk with a therapist who could help you sort things out. You could even help choose the therapist to make sure they are the right fit for you.

It is important to check in with yourself from time to time, asking "How am I feeling?" "Am I happy overall?" "Are there things that I need to talk about or spend some time thinking through?" Here are 3 tips for making sure you maintain good mental health:

1. Self-care (taking care of yourself): Think about 3 things that you enjoy doing and try to do those things consistently. Examples might be: painting your nails a color you like, putting your hair in a protective style so you feel good about your hair, taking a break from your phone or social media, organizing your room up how you like it so you're comfortable in it, etc.

2. Outlets: Make sure you have healthy ways to express your emotions and discharge stress. Examples could be: playing a sport, writing in a journal, drawing, doing art, going for a walk or jogging, playing with a pet, talking to a parent or a friend, praying, etc.

3. Coping Skills: How do you handle big feelings? Make sure you identify at least 3 ways to deal with strong emotions. Examples could be: snuggling in a warm blanket or with a favorite stuffed animal to soothe yourself as you think about what's

bothering you, crying, listening to music that might help you feel better, saying positive affirmations to remind yourself that it's okay to feel what you are feeling and remind yourself that you will be okay and will get through it. Taking deep breaths when dealing with intense feelings is also very helpful.

Try to remember that you are still young and trying to figure things out! Sometimes you're going to make mistakes, get it wrong, people will disappoint you, and life can be stressful! But- you are not alone and you have a whole family and social support system who are there when you need them. Also, you are capable of taking good care of your mental health if you use some of the strategies above. And if you get stuck, there is always help available to you. Remember to take good care of yourself!

Love,
Aunt/Coach Bynia

La La's Lessons

As I was reflecting on my childhood and the people who have shaped me into the person I am today, I could not help but think of my maternal grandmother, whom you knew as La La. Growing up, I had the privilege of living with her and learning from her. She was a wise and loving woman, and I am grateful for the lessons she taught me.

La La was a strong woman who taught me many valuable lessons about life. One of the things she often told me was that I should have pursued a career in law because I "sure love to have the last word." While I never did become a lawyer, I do appreciate her encouragement to speak up for myself and fight for what I believe in.

Another lesson she taught me was that food can be used as a tool to get a kid to stop talking. She would always say, "let your food stop your mouth." While this may not be the healthiest approach, I do understand the sentiment behind it.

La La also taught me that not everything is meant to be understood. I still do not fully understand her saying, "I'm the liar and you're the pretty girl," but I know that she had her reasons for saying it.

Despite her quirky sayings and beliefs, La La taught me many invaluable things. She taught me the love of family is boundless and that only God has greater importance than family. She also taught me the value of time management, as she was able to get fifty 'leven people ready in her one-bathroom home and be where they needed to be on time.

La La was a woman of service. She served her family, her God, and her community. Some of my best memories were created in her kitchen, where we enjoyed delicious meals, great conversations, fun games, witnessed history, welcomed new additions, and so much more.

She taught me that the people you care for are worth your time and support. She had been there for every monumental and minuscule moment in my life. She also showed me that it cost absolutely nothing to make a person feel welcome. La La accepted SO many people into the fold and her family.

Most importantly, La La taught me the power of prayer. Without a doubt, some of my blessings and favor are because I had a grandmother who prays for me. She also taught me that rest is one of the best medicines. Sick, cranky, or bored, it really did not matter. Her cure was always the same: go to sleep.

You often talked about wanting to become an old person because old people were rich. La La would always give you a few dollars whenever she saw you, and you thought your pockets were "flooded." While she may not have been rich in terms of money, she was rich in love and wisdom. She did not mind sharing her wealth with anyone who needed it.

Here is a little gem for you, you can thank me later (wink). No matter how much time we spend with our loved ones, the finite nature of time means it never feels like enough. Now that La La has passed, my memories of her are even more precious to me, reminding me of the importance of creating as many memories as possible and cherishing them, because ultimately, those memories will be all we have left. I am grateful that you had the chance to know La La and make special moments with her, and I hope that your 12 years of memories of her will bring you as much happiness and comfort as mine do for me.

XOXO,

Mom

God Bless You

Dear Joelle,

A blessing is one way of asking for God's divine favor to rest on others.

Lord bless Joelle and make Joelle a blessing!

Lord keep Joelle safe on this journey called life and grant Joelle the desires of her heart as they line up with your will for her life.

Lord may you be pleased with all that Joelle does and be merciful and compassionate to her.

Lord give Joelle your peace not according to how the dictionary defines peace as the absence of conflict but rather your peace which is the inner calmness and confidence that you as her Heavenly Father are in control.

Lord may Joelle trust Jesus as Savior and Holy Spirit as the power within her.

Lord may your goodness and mercy follow Joelle all the days of her life. Amen!

Grace and Peace my precious great-niece,
Love Aunt Vivian

Your Dad Adores You

As I write this, I cannot help but think about the relationship I had with my own father growing up. It was a sore spot for me, and watching you interact with your dad has been a source of my healing. I am so grateful that you have a dad who shares his heart and lends his hand, rather than just sharing his DNA as my father did. Not every child is as lucky as you are to have a dad like him, and not every girl is given the opportunity to be a daddy's girl. So, I urge you to appreciate him, even when it is difficult.

I admire your dad for being actively involved in your life, even when you push him away. He loves you and wants nothing but the best for you. He is there to love and protect you, to help you develop and flourish into the amazing person you are becoming. As difficult as he may be at times, please offer him a little grace and understanding. He is a first-time girl dad, and he is still learning to navigate a world that is new to him. When you were younger, it was easier for him when you enjoyed simple things like giving him facials and hand massages, singing and dancing with him, or visiting his mother, your Grandma Vivian. But now that you are maturing, he is trying to find his place in your world, and that can be challenging.

As someone who was once a teenage girl, I understand you. We naturally bond over food and fashion, your feelings, and your friends. Your dad, on the other hand, is still trying to find common ground and mutual interests with you. As you become more independent and mature, please remember that you will always be your dad's little lady. He still looks at you with the same heart-shaped eyes that he had the day you were born.

I encourage you to spend time with your dad, just the two of you. Cement your bond and make memories that you will cherish forever. Talk to him about anything and everything, he is literally walking news that you may or may not be able to use. He can offer you a different perspective and a man's point of view. If you are ever in doubt about how much your dad loves and values you, think about how hard he works daily to provide for the family and how invested he is in your dreams.

I know that sometimes your dad may press you harder than you would like. It is because he wants you to be better than both of us, to go further than we did, and to accomplish more than you can even imagine. As you get older, you will understand the method to his madness. But until then, I will be your tag team partner, helping you navigate this beautiful but sometimes complicated relationship with your dad.

Always remember that your dad loves you more than anything in this world, and I do too.

XOXO
Mom

The World Needs You

Dear Joelle,

I hope this letter finds you well. I wanted to take a moment to tell you how special, beautiful and loved you are. You are a precious gift to this world, and I feel so lucky to know you. I am constantly amazed by your kind heart, your infectious smile, and your unwavering spirit. You bring joy and light wherever you go, and I am grateful to have you in my life.

Please know that you are loved deeply and unconditionally. You have a significant place in the hearts of those around you, and your presence makes this world a better place. Your smile brightens up any room, and your kindness touches the hearts of everyone you meet.

As you navigate through life, always remember that you are capable of achieving anything you set your mind to. Your potential is limitless, and I have no doubt that you will accomplish great things. So, Joelle, keep shining your light and spreading your love. You are a beautiful soul, and the world needs more people like you. Know that you are special, loved, and cherished, always.

With love and admiration,
Aunt Cari

10 Things You Need To Keep Doing

No matter how old you get, it is important to stay true to yourself. Here are 10 things you should continue doing:

1. Listening to your favorite music and singing out loud at the top of your lungs. Music is a faithful companion. Whether you are happy or sad, there is a song that can express your feelings and make you feel better.

2. Dancing and not just the two-step, move your body like nobody is watching. Your dad is a great example of this. He is capable of having a dance party alone. You should continue to follow in his footsteps.

3. Liking what you like, no matter what the trend is. Whether it is your fashion choices or the movies you watch on repeat, never let anyone tell you what you should like. Be true to yourself and embrace your individuality.

4. Owning your spot in your sibling circle, JC3. Having two older brothers must feel like having three fathers. It can tell it gets overwhelming at times, but you do not let their actions dictate your

own. Instead, you assert yourself and stand up for your beliefs with both of your brothers.

5. Trying new things, such as learning to cook pancakes. With persistence, you will eventually make the perfect batch with the ideal fluffiness and crispiness. The process of trying and failing is how you grow and learn.

6. Laughing out loud. At times, I overhear you laughing so much in your room that you end up coughing. It is crucial not to be too serious about life or yourself. Keep searching for humor in your daily routine.

7. Taking care of your body. You only have one, so make sure to keep up with your skincare routine, dental hygiene, and exercise regimen. Your physical health is important, and an annual check-up with your doctor can help you catch any potential issues before they become major problems.

8. Spending time with the people you love. Whether it is your family or your closest friends, being around people you enjoy makes the day more enjoyable, which is why days when your school/work best friend is absent tend to feel longer.

9. Going outside. When we are children, we view the outdoors as a magical place with endless possibilities for exploration and adventure. However, as we grow older and busier, outside

often becomes a mere means of transportation to get from one place to another. Whether it is taking a leisurely walk, sitting quietly and listening to the sounds of nature, taking a dip in the pool, or gathering around a fire pit to enjoy s'mores with friends and family, spend time outdoors.

10. Giving out compliments. You have a knack for recognizing the positive traits in people and expressing your admiration. Keep spreading positivity with your compliments whenever you can. You never know how much of an impact it may have on someone's day, and you will also experience a sense of satisfaction from making others feel good about themselves.

Remember these things, Ells, and never stop doing them. They can make a huge difference in your life and the lives of those around you.

XOXO,
Mom

Brothers Are Not So Bad

Dear Joelle,

Looking back it is hard to believe that I have known you your whole life. You have always been such a joy to be around. I remember all the dancing, singing, and flipping you would do when you were younger and it makes me smile. You are able to brighten any room. Never let anyone dim your light.

When I was your age I was often annoyed by my older brother so I have to imagine that is multiplied for you since you have two brothers but trust me it has its advantages. People will come in and out of your life but siblings are forever. You share so much more than your parents. You share memories and life experiences(and inside jokes) that reassure you that you are never alone. Growing up with brothers gives you insight into what men go through and will help you be more compassionate and understanding of others. So next time you yearn for your brothers to leave you alone know that the positives of having brothers far outweigh the aggravation.

I believe in you always.

Love,
Aunt Toni

Love Your Body

Your dad and I tell you often that you are beautiful, but the question is, do you see it? Do you believe it? Your view of yourself is what matters most.

I know that sometimes it can be hard to see the beauty in yourself, especially when you focus on your flaws. I remember as a teen, I was not a fan of my body or the way I looked. I would tell myself negative comments about my skin color, my size, my nose shape, my ears, and my smile. But over time, I learned that being kind to myself and giving myself compliments was important. I realized that I had enough critics in the world and did not need to be another name on the list.

It is important to remember that beauty comes in many forms and is not just physical. You have so many unique qualities, talents, and personality traits that make you beautiful. Embrace the things that make you different and bask in them. They are what make you special.

Your self-esteem and body image go hand in hand. It is important to pay attention to how you feel about the way you look and what you say to yourself when you look in the mirror. Do you focus more on the features that you like or the ones that you think are flaws? Remember, even if you are an esteemed person, you will not love every single thing about yourself every single day. Some days you will be harder on yourself than you should be. However, if most days you are happy with the way you look, then you are winning and have a positive body image.

I want you to know that your body is so much more than its appearance. It carries you through life and deserves to be respected and treated well. Eat healthy, exercise often, and rest properly-be better than I am in these areas. Show your gratitude for all that it does for you.

Finally, You will forever be a 10 since you were born on the 10th. You come from a family of baddies, and beauty is in your DNA. The "B" in Bridgers stands for beautiful, and you should believe it and own it.

XOXO,
Mom

Be Encouraged

Start each new day in a positive way. Say these affirmations in front of a mirror out loud or meditate on them (say them to yourself with your eyes closed).

I Am Me
I Am Smart
I Am Beautiful
I Am Kind
I Am Strong
I Am Loved
I Am filled with confidence
I Am Healthy
I Am comfortable saying No! As a complete sentence.

Jo Jo,

1. You are uniquely gifted. No one else in the world can do exactly what you do in exactly the way you do it. That is amazing.

2. Your skin is a gorgeous shade of brown. It sparkles like gold.

3. Mistakes are not the end of you. Challenges are not the end of you. You learn from them and you get better because of them. You are powerful.

Aynae

The Value of Friends

The saying, "family over everything," is often used to emphasize the importance of familial relationships. However, this phrase implies that familial relationships are superior to friendships. Know that friendships can be just as essential to your life. The main difference between these two relationships is that you choose your friends, whereas family is chosen for you. As you know, some of my closest friends are actually my cousins, so I feel like I have the best of both worlds - friends within my family. But I know not everyone has this luxury. Surrounding yourself with people who uplift you and make you feel good is what matter most. This may mean prioritizing your friends over your family, which is okay.

It is beneficial to distinguish between acquaintances and friends. An acquaintance is someone you are familiar with, but not necessarily someone you have a close relationship with. In contrast, a friend is someone who is compassionate, respectful, trustworthy, dependable, supportive, and fun. A true friend accepts you for who you are without judgment, and they want to see you succeed. It is important to pay attention to how your friends treat others, as this is a reflection of their integrity. While it is normal for friends to sometimes partake in some foolery, a true friend would never encourage you to do something that would harm you or others. Generally, if you strive to be the caliber of friend you desire to have, you will be a good friend.

It is okay to make new friends and keep old ones - the length of a friendship does not necessarily determine its strength. Making new friends does not mean that you are neglecting your old ones. However, not all friends are meant to be lifers. Some friends may be temporary, while others may blossom into lifelong friendships. The key is to measure friendships by quality, not quantity. A few genuine friends who positively impact your life are more valuable than a large group of fairweather friends. In ten years, your friend group will likely include different individuals than it does today, do not stress it, as long as your circle consists of people you genuinely relate to, who support you, and accept you for who you are, consider yourself blessed. And regardless of how many friendships you may gain or lose, you can count on me to forever remain a steadfast and dependable friend to you.

XOXO,
Mom

My Friend, Your Angel

Precious Joelle,

Happy 13th Birthday! Look at you now! You are growing into a perfect, sweet, and smart young teenager. May God bless you with all of your dreams and aspirations. It's celebration time!

Now I would like to tell you a little about me and your grandmother, Dorothy Lena Bridgers. We met working in the Federal Government, in 1971, for the Social Security Administration. We hit it off from day one. We became friends that grew into best friends (my BFF). We sometimes dressed alike. We often traveled together to places like New York, the famous underground located in Atlanta, GA, and Atlantic City in New Jersey. We also flew to the Bahamas on a wonderful vacation. We even had a pool party in Columbia, MD where we invited our friends and family. We had a blast! We also worshipped together along with your great-grandmother, Mother Bridgers, at Shiloh Community Church. Dorothy (known as Sister) and I would take my 3-year-old daughter at the time named La Keshia, and your cousin Robin who was 8 months old to church with us. We both were Christians, loved the Lord, and became more like sisters. Later, on November 06, 1976, your mother was born. I became a first-time godmother of a precious beautiful baby girl, Kia Deneen Woodson, and was called "affectionately", Aunt Lamour.

Next, it is time to talk about your precious grandmother. I can remember our last conversation on the phone. She proudly told me that your mother was pregnant with you, her "Little Popsicle". She was eagerly anticipating the birth of you, her precious granddaughter, Joelle Leah Milan Clark. So unexpectedly, shortly right after that, she became ill and later went home to be with God in Heaven. Most importantly, your grandmother loved her grandchildren. At that time, she had her two adorable grandsons, Jaylen and Jace. They were her heart. She loved her grandchildren to the moon and back. Your grandmother is still looking down smiling and her legacy will live on forever in the hearts of all who loved her dearly. Again, "Happy 13th Birthday" I am sending you lots of hugs and kisses from your Beautiful! precious grandmother and your Auntie Lamour.

Joelle:
J-oy
O-ptimistic
E-ncourager
L-oveable
L-aughter
E-arnest (sincere)

Enjoy Your day!

Have fun and lots of laughter!

Love and Blessings,
Auntie Lamour

Thirteen (BIG) Little Things

Many people seem to think that the BIG moments and grand gestures are the most wonderful. They imagine themselves traveling to exotic locations, receiving lavish gifts, or achieving great accomplishments. And while those things are certainly exciting, in my opinion, it is the simple things that make life the sweetest.

It is the little moments, the unexpected surprises, and the small gestures of kindness that truly make life worth living. Whether it is at the hands of another or your own self-care, the little things matter A LOT. And most often, they become the BIG things.

Imagine us sitting on the beach, enjoying virgin Strawberry Daiquiris on a hot summer day. It is a little thing, but it is a moment that we will remember for years to come. When I am more seasoned and you are an adult, we will look back on said memory with fondness and a smile.

Life is full of these little moments that we often take for granted. We get so caught up in our busy lives that we forget to slow down and enjoy the little things. But it is these moments that can bring us the most joy and happiness.

Here are 13 (BIG) little things that I think you should experience at least once in your life:

1. Watching the sunrise or sunset over the ocean.

2. Seeing a rainbow after a storm.

3. Laughing so hard that you cry or your stomach hurts.

4. Getting a back hug from someone you love.

5. Eating a meal or dessert so delicious that you dance in your seat.

6. Hearing an old song that triggers good times.

7. Receiving a call or text from the person you were just thinking about.

8. Falling in love with a swoon-worthy book character.

9. Spending a day doing nothing but relaxing and enjoying your own company.

10. Getting a massage or spa treatment.

11. Enjoying comforting silence with someone you love.

12. Hearing an inspiring testimony that gives you hope.

13. Holding a sleeping baby on your shoulder.

These may seem like small things, but they can make a big difference in your life. Do not ever get so busy you forget to enjoy what stirs your soul and take the time to appreciate the little things. Life is too short to only focus on the big moments. The little things are what make life truly sweet.

XOXO,
Mom

Always Remember...

Joelle, as you blossom into a young woman always remember:

YOU are beautiful, so love yourself unconditionally.

Life can be challenging, but you can do the impossible.

Whatever you do, do it with Love and Compassion.

Never discredit yourself, because you are more than enough.

Every day is a gift, so enjoy every moment.

Demicca

Facts About My Favorite Daughter

Did you know that you were born on a Saturday? It is a fun fact that I wanted to be aware of. Your birth was one of the most precious moments in my life. Aunt Nikki suggested your first middle name Leah, which means delicate, and I chose your second middle name Milan, which means kind, loving, and gracious. Both names are so fitting for your personality.

I want to share some more memories with you that I cherish. Days after your grandmother woke from her coma, she asked to rub my growing belly that was carrying you. It was such a beautiful moment, and I knew then that you would bring joy to our family.

When you were a baby, someone looking in your direction would send you into a crying fit. You were so delicate and sensitive. But you were also brave. You took your first vacation and flight at three months of age when we went to Disney in Orlando, Florida. You were a champion even then!

We have lived at five different addresses since your birth, but no matter where we go, you always make it feel like home. You started walking before your first birthday, and your brother Jace helped you take your first steps. He was so proud of you!

We tried to give you a nickname, but it morphed into a few. Some people call you Jo Jo, while others call you Joey. I fluctuate between Ells and Baby Girl. For a while, you were known as Shadyboots. Even though we called you Popsicle before you were born, it never stuck after you graced us with your presence.

Kobi and Olivia are your cousins, but they were your very first friends. I kept the three of you during the weekday when you were all toddlers. You pulled your first loose tooth, and I remember being shocked that you pulled it on your own! You were so excited and impressed with yourself!

Pitch Perfect and *Frozen* were two of your favorite movies. You knew all of the words to every song. You took ballet, tap, and gymnastics classes, attended a soccer clinic, and joined the dance and cheer team at school, but running is the only recreational activity that has held your interest long-term. I am proud of you for finding something that you enjoy.

And finally, I wanted to remind you that you are my FAVORITE daughter and I love you more than words can express.

XOXO,
Mom

Enjoy Each Day Of Every Year

Jo Jo,

What I would tell my 13-year-old self is that turning 13 brings so much to a young black girl. Emotions, questions, concerns, and thoughts you never thought you would have. With all that I know you feel like chaos is going on in your mind let alone the world and you are unsure of yourself and what is to come.

Knowing what I know now, I would tell myself to calm all the chaos and listen to YOU and be true to YOUR thoughts, not outsiders. Do not think you are in competition with everyone; you are only in competition with yourself. Keep this quote in mind:

"I am black and beautiful and I am me and being me is perfect " -Kina H.

Don't let others place doubt in YOU. Enjoy your 13 years old self and what you enjoy doing. Life is too short to not enjoy your new age. One day you are 13 and the next, you are 21 in a blink of an eye. And you will wonder where did the time go. So enjoy you and each new day.

Love,
Aunt Kina

It Is True, It Is So

Dear, heavenly father Jehovah, we just humbly come before you and we thank you for blessing us with Joelle. We just pray that you continue to bless her and let her know that she is loved and smart and beautiful inside and out. We ask that you protect her and always direct and guide her steps. Thank you for letting her shine her light on our family, we are truly blessed. Amen. Amen. Amen.

Love, Auntie Candy

To The Future (23) You

As I look back on the last ten years of your life, I cannot help but feel grateful for all the milestones you have hit. From turning 16, 18, and 21 to earning your driver's license and walking across the stage to receive your high school and college degrees. Ells, you have accomplished a lot. Throughout it all, we have been there to cheer you on and support you. We are so very proud of you Baby Girl!

One of the highlights of your high school and college experiences was being a member of the track team. Not only did you learn valuable life lessons about determination and grit, but you also gained friendships that will last a lifetime. Being away at college gave you a new level of independence, and while it was challenging at times, it helped you grow into the self-assured woman standing before me. I see you, beautiful! You are such an amazing person who has done some pretty awesome things!

Looking ahead to the next ten years, there is a list of ten things you should consider accomplishing. These include building multiple streams of income, traveling regularly, establishing financial stability, sharing your story, nurturing relationships with loved ones, learning a new language, maintaining physical fitness and mental health, taking time for yourself, and being in love with yourself.

As I reflect on your past and think about your future, I want you to realize the importance of having a vision for your life. By visualizing what you want and taking intentional actions to make it happen, you can manifest your dreams into reality. Remember that while there will be challenges and obstacles along the way, with determination and dedication, you can accomplish anything you set your mind to. You can do all things through Christ who strengthens you.-Philippians 4:13 So dream big, work hard, and never give up on your dreams. I believe in you!

XOXO,
Mom

List of Contributors

Ada Gaines
Alita Credell
Aynae Lee
Bynia Reed
Candice Clark
Cari Bridgers
Courtney Smith
Demicca Ross
Kina Heflin
Lamour Anderson
Lenora (Gail) Bridgers
Linda Carmody
Michelle Woodson
Nikki Joyner
Robin Jones
Taylor Joyner
Terri Grant
Toni Snead
Vivian Snead